LIVING
IN THE
READER'S WORLD

Book 1

CAMBRIDGE
THE ADULT EDUCATION COMPANY
888 Seventh Avenue New York, N.Y. 10106

LIVING
in the Reader's World

Executive Editor: Brian Schenk

Project Editor: Dennis Mendyk

Contributing Editor: Laura Daly

ISBN   0–8428–9514–0

9 8 7 6 5 4 3

CONTENTS

SIGNS AND ADS

LISTS AND TABLES

APPENDIX: Unit Outlines and Word Lists   147

IMPORTANT NOTE TO THE INSTRUCTOR

Please read the appendix to this book before you begin any instruction. The appendix begins on page 147.

UNIT 1

Think about signs.

Most signs have words on them.

But some don't.

Here is a road sign.

What does it mean?

How can you tell?

Here is another sign.

What does this sign mean?

How can you tell?

These signs are pictures.

The pictures tell you what the signs mean.

TRYING IT OUT

What do these signs mean?

PUTTING WORDS IN THEIR PLACE

Fill in the blanks.
Use the words in the list.

means
It
road
words
tells

1. This is a _____ sign.

2. _____ has a picture on it.

3. It does not have _____ on it.

4. The picture _____ you what the sign _____ .

LOOKING AT WORDS

Fill in the blanks.

Most signs have w__rds on them.

But some signs are p__ctures.

The p__ctures tell you wh__t the signs mean.

TRYING IT ON YOUR OWN

Look for picture signs.

What do they mean?

How can you tell?

UNIT 2

Many signs have pictures and words on them.

Look at this sign.

The picture and the words mean the same thing.

They mean you can not turn left.

But look at this sign.

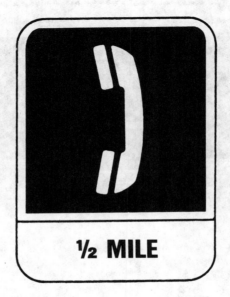

½ MILE

The picture tells you one thing.

It tells you about a telephone.

The words tell you another thing.

They tell you where the telephone is.

Here is a store sign.

What is the store's name?

What does the store sell?

How can you tell?

Here is another store sign.

What is the store's name?

What does the store sell?

How can you tell?

Many signs have words and pictures on them.

Sometimes the words and pictures mean the same thing.

Sometimes they don't.

TRYING IT OUT

Look at these signs.

Do the words and the pictures mean the same thing?

Print <u>YES</u> if they do.

Print <u>NO</u> if they don't.

_____   _____   _____

_____

PUTTING WORDS IN THEIR PLACE

Fill in the blanks.

Use the words in the list.

sells

sign

picture

name

1. This is a store _____.

2. The store's _____ is "Al's."

3. The store _____ fish.

4. The _____ on the sign tells you what the store sells.

LOOKING AT WORDS

Fill in the blanks.

Many signs h__ve pictures and w__rds on them.

Sometimes the pictures and w__rds mean the same th__ng.

Sometimes they d__n't mean the same th__ng.

TRYING IT ON YOUR OWN

Look for words and pictures on signs.

Do the words and pictures mean the same thing?

Do the pictures tell you something about the words?

UNIT 3

You may not know all the words on a sign.

But a picture can give you a good clue about what the sign is for.

Look at this store sign.

The store's name is "Marv's."

You may not know the other words.

But can you tell what the store sells?

Does the picture give you a good clue?

The store sells flowers.

Here is another sign.

COMBUSTIBLE

You may not know the word on the sign.

But the picture gives you a clue.

What does the picture tell you?

What does the sign mean?

A picture can give you a good clue about what a sign is for.

But there are other clues.

Look at the sign in this picture.

There are no words on it.

Can you tell what the sign is?

The sign's shape gives you a clue.

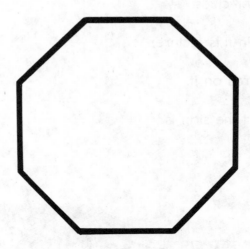

The sign's place gives you a clue.

You may not know all the words on a sign.

But you can look for clues.

Sometimes a picture gives a good clue.

Sometimes the sign's shape gives a good clue.

Sometimes the sign's place gives a good clue.

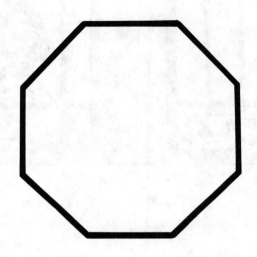

TRYING IT OUT

Can you tell what these signs are for?

Use the picture, shape, and place clues.

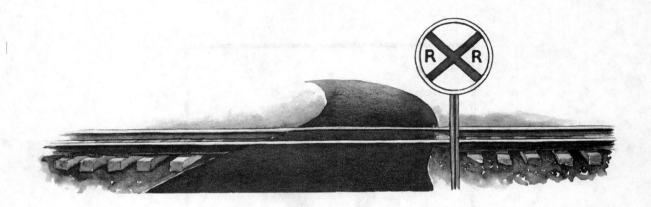

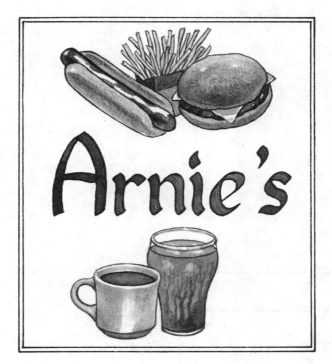

PUTTING WORDS IN THEIR PLACE

Fill in the blanks.

Use the words in the list.

look
shape
know
clue
give

1. You may not _____ all the words on a sign.

2. But you can _____ for clues.

3. Pictures can _____ you a clue.

4. The sign's _____ can give you a clue.

5. The sign's place can give you a _____ .

LOOKING AT WORDS

Fill in the blanks.

You may not know all the w__rds on a s__gn.

But there are clues you c__n use.

A p__cture c__n give you a g____d clue.

The s__gn's shape c__n give you a clue.

The s__gn's place c__n give you a clue.

TRYING IT ON YOUR OWN

Look for the clues on signs.

Can you think of other sign clues?

UNIT 4   (REVIEW)

Match the words and the signs.

1.   NO LEFT TURN   ___

2.   STOP

3.   TELEPHONE   ___

4.   ONE WAY

___

5.   NO U TURN

___

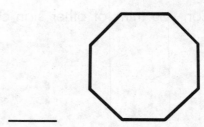

___

___

Fill in the blanks.

Use the words in the list.

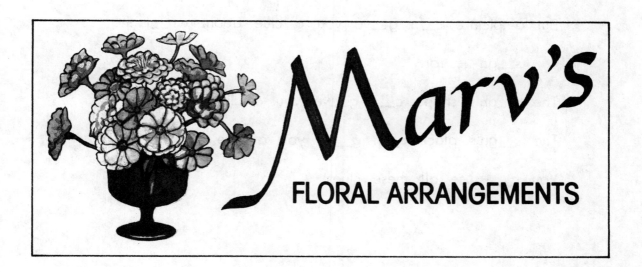

sells

picture

name

sign

store

1. This is a store _____ .

2. The store's _____ is "Marv's."

3. The _____ on the sign tells you what the _____
    sells.

4. The store _____ flowers.

Fill in the blanks.

Think about signs.

You may not kn__w all the w__rds on a s__gn.

But a picture c__n g__ve you a clue about wh__t the

s__gn is for.

The s__gn's shape c__n g__ve you a clue.

The s__gn's place c__n g__ve you a clue.

You c__n use all these clues.

UNIT 5

Think about ads.

Most ads are used to sell you something.

Look at this ad.

What is "Zippy"?

How can you tell?

What does the ad say?

Some ads are used to tell you something.

Look at this ad.

What does the ad say?

What does the picture show you?

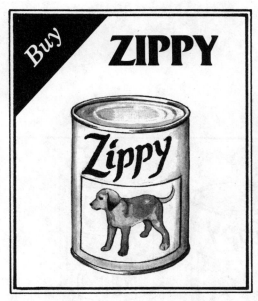 

Ads are like signs in many ways.

Many signs have words and pictures on them.

Many ads have words and pictures in them.

Signs and ads can be used to tell you something.

They can be used to sell things.

TRYING IT OUT

What do these ads say?

Use the pictures for clues.

PUTTING WORDS IN THEIR PLACE

Fill in the blanks.

Use the words in the list.

be
something
Ads
have
ways

1. _____ are like signs in many _____ .

2. Many ads _____ words and pictures in them.

3. Signs and ads can _____ used to tell you

    _____ .

LOOKING AT WORDS

Fill in the blanks.

Think about ads.

Ads are l__ke signs in many w__ys.

Signs and ads c__n be used to t__ll you s__mething.

They c__n be used to s__ll you s__mething.

TRYING IT ON YOUR OWN

Look for some ads.

Who uses ads?

Why are ads used?

Where can you find ads?

UNIT 6

Pictures are used in many ads.

They tell about the things in the ad.

Look at this word.

Do you know what "Fud's" is?

You don't?

Now look at the word.

Now do you know what "Fud's" is?

The picture tells you what "Fud's" is.

"Fud's" is the name of a soda.

The words tell you something about "Fud's."

They tell you "Fud's" tastes good.

Look at this word.

YES

You know what this word means.

But look at this ad.

Does "YES" mean the same thing in the ad?

What does "YES" mean in the ad?

How can you tell?

You may not know all the words in an ad.

But a picture in the ad can give you a clue about the words.

Look at this ad.

You may not know what "exterminators" are.

But the picture gives you a clue.

Exterminators kill bugs.

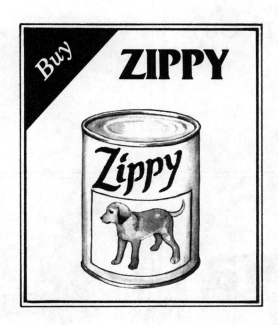

Pictures are used in many ads.

They tell about the things in the ad.

They give you clues about the words in the ad.

They give you clues about what the ad means.

TRYING IT OUT

Look at this ad.

1. What is "Java"?

2. What do the words say about "Java"?

3. Can you tell what "Java" is from looking at the picture?

4. Is this ad used to tell you something or to sell you something?

PUTTING WORDS IN THEIR PLACE

Fill in the blanks.

Use the words in the list.

"Fud's"
something
name
ad
picture

1. This is an _____ for "Fud's."

2. _____ is the _____ of a soda.

3. The _____ tells you what "Fud's" is.

4. The words tell you _____ about "Fud's."

LOOKING AT WORDS

Fill in the blanks.

P__ctures are used in many ads.

P__ctures can tell ab____t the th__gs in the ad.

They can g__ve you a clue ab____t w__rds in the ad.

They can g__ve you a clue ab____t wh__t the ad means.

TRYING IT ON YOUR OWN

Look at some ads.

Do pictures tell you what the ads are for?

Do pictures give you clues about the words in the ads?

UNIT 7

Look at the ad.

Then look at the questions.

1. What is the ad about?

2. What does the ad say?

3. Why is the ad used?

The answers to these three questions are important.

The answers add up to the ad's <u>main point</u>.

The main point is the main thing the ad says.

The main point is the reason the ad is used.

Look at the answers to the questions.

Fud's *means good taste.*

1. What is the ad about?

   The ad is about "Fud's" soda.

2. What does the ad say?

   The ad says "Fud's" tastes good.

3. Why is the ad used?

   The ad is used to sell "Fud's" soda.

The three answers add up to the ad's main point.

Here is another ad.

Look at the ad.

Then look at the questions and answers.

1. What is the ad about?

    The ad is about drinking and driving.

2. What does the ad say?

    The ad says drinking and driving may kill you.

3. Why is the ad used?

    The ad is used to tell you not to drink and drive.

The three answers add up to the ad's main point.

The main point of an ad is the main thing the ad says.

The main point is the reason the ad is used.

You can use these questions to find the main point:

1. What is the ad about?

2. What does the ad say?

3. Why is the ad used?

The answers to these questions add up to the main point.

TRYING IT OUT

Look at each ad.

Answer the questions about it.

Do the answers add up to the main point?

1. What is the ad about?

2. What does the ad say?

3. Why is the ad used?

1. What is the ad about?

2. What does the ad say?

3. Why is the ad used?

PUTTING WORDS IN THEIR PLACE

Fill in the blanks.

Use the words in the list.

says
is
ad
used
good

This is an ————— for "Fud's" soda.

The ad ————— "Fud's" tastes —————.

The ad is ————— to sell "Fud's" soda.

This ————— the main point of the ad.

LOOKING AT WORDS

Fill in the blanks.

The main point of an ad is the m__ __n thing
the ad says.

The m__ __n p__ __nt is the reason the ad is used.

You can use three quest__ __ns to find the m__ __n
p__ __t:

1. What is the ad ab__ __t?

2. Wh__t does the ad s__y?

3. Why is the ad used?

The answers to these qu__st__ __ns add up to the
m__ __n p__ __nt.

TRYING IT ON YOUR OWN

Listen to ads on radio or TV.

Answer the three questions about the ads.

What is the main point of each ad?

UNIT 8   (REVIEW)

Look at the ad.

Then fill in the blanks.

1. This is an ad for a —————— .

2. The name of the soap is —————— .

3. The ad says the soap is for —————— .

4. The ad is used to get you to —————— the soap.

Fill in the blanks.

Use the words in the list.

have
something
ways
to
like
them
can

Ads are _____ signs in many _____ .

Many ads and signs _____ words and pictures on _____ .

Ads and signs _____ be used to tell you _____ .

They can be used _____ sell you something.

Fill in the blanks.

Here is a way to find the main p__ __nt of an ad.

L__ __k at the ad.

Then answ__r these three qu__st__ __ns:

1. What is the ad ab__ __t?

2. What d__ __ __s the ad say?

3. Why is the ad used?

The answers to these qu__st__ __ns add up to the
    m__ __n p__ __nt.

UNIT 9

Think about lists.

Lists are used for many reasons.

Lists can be used to show a group of things.

Look at this list.

<u>Things to buy at the store</u>

milk
butter
eggs
soap
coffee

The list shows a group of things.

It shows a group of things to buy at the store.

Lists can make something easier to understand.

Here is a road sign.

It has a list on it.

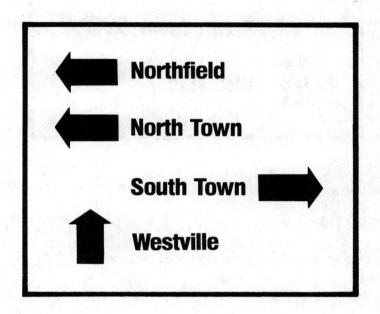

The sign has a list of towns on it.

The arrows tell you where the towns are.

This is what the sign means:

Turn left to go to Northfield.
Turn left to go to North Town.
Turn right to go to South Town.
Go straight to go to Westville.

The list and the arrows make the sign easy to understand.

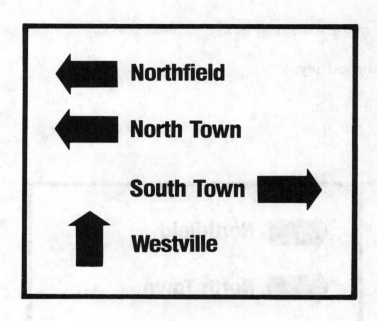

The list makes it easier for you to find where you want to go.

All you have to do is find the name of the town.

Then go the way the arrow points.

Some ads have lists in them.

Look at this ad.

What is the ad for?

What is listed in the ad?

Lists have many uses.

They can be used to show a group of things.

They can be used to make things easier to understand.

They can be used to make things easier to find.

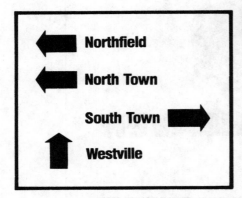

TRYING IT OUT

Look at the ad.

Then answer the questions about it.

SALE!

MEN'S WORLD STORE
46 Mars Highway
Northfield

We have a **SALE** on all

- belts
- hats
- ties
- shoes
- socks

in our store!

Come in and **SAVE** at

MEN'S WORLD!

---

1. What is this ad for?

2. What is listed in the ad?

3. Why are the things listed?

PUTTING WORDS IN THEIR PLACE

Fill in the blanks.

Use the words in the list.

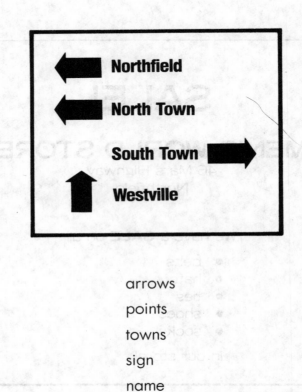

arrows

points

towns

sign

name

1. This road sign has a list of _____ on it.

2. The _____ tell you where the towns are.

3. All you have to do is find the _____ of the town.

4. Then go the way the arrow _____.

5. The list and the arrows make the _____ easy to understand.

LOOKING AT WORDS

Fill in the blanks.

Lists have m__ny uses.

They c__n be used to show a gr___p of th__ngs.

They c__n be used to make th__ngs easier to
    und__rst__nd.

They c__n be used to make th__ngs easier to f__nd.

TRYING IT ON YOUR OWN

Look for a list in an ad.

What is in the list?

Does the list make the ad easier to understand?

UNIT 10

Look at this list.

eggs
milk
butter
sugar
salt
flour

The things in the list are foods.

But why are the foods listed?

What is the main point of this list?

You can't tell what the list is for.

There are no clues to tell you what the list is for.

Now look at the list.

<u>Foods you need to make a cake</u>

eggs

milk

butter

sugar

salt

flour

Now it is easier to tell what the list is for.

The words at the top of the list tell you.

It is a list of foods you need to make a cake.

The words at the top of a list are the <u>heading</u> of the list.

Here is another list.

Does the heading give you the main point of the list?

<u>Things to do today</u>

1. Go to the store.
2. Make a cake.
3. Look for the radio.

This is a list of things to do today.

The heading tells you this.

The heading gives you the main point of the list.

Sometimes the way the list is used gives you a clue about the main point.

Look at this list.

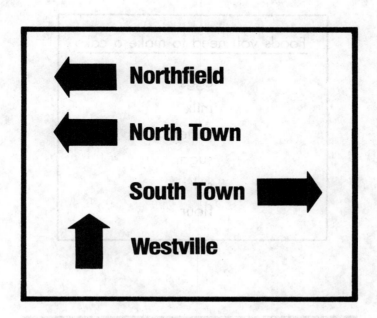

The list is on a road sign.

The arrows tell you where the towns are.

There is no heading on the list.

But you know the main point of the list.

The way the list is used gives you a clue about the main point.

Use clues to find the main point of a list.

Sometimes the heading gives you a clue about the main point.

Sometimes the way the list is used gives you a clue.

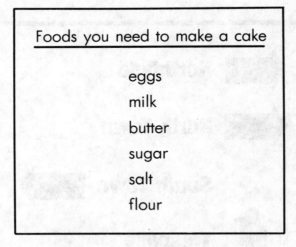

Foods you need to make a cake

eggs

milk

butter

sugar

salt

flour

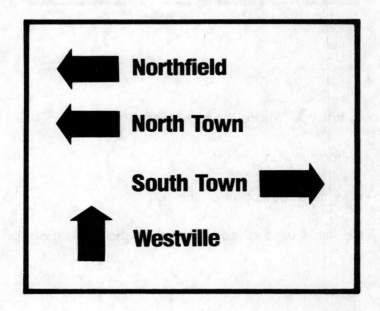

TRYING IT OUT

Look at each list.

What is the main point of the list?

Use the clues.

TOP THREE SONGS

1. "Looking for Clues"
2. "They Say You Know"
3. "Three Reasons to Go"

NORTH TOWN MALL

Al's Fish Store

Marv's Flowers

Art's TV Heaven

Ace Exterminators

Burger Heaven

North Town Food Store

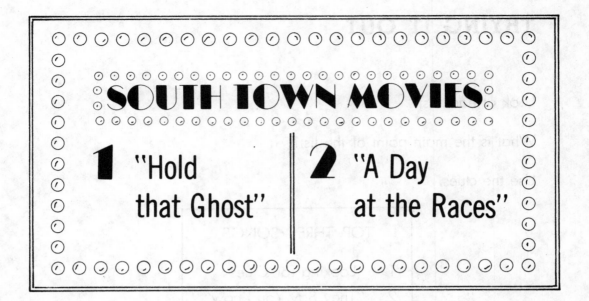

SOUTH TOWN MOVIES

1 "Hold that Ghost"

2 "A Day at the Races"

NORTH POINT

MAIN PLACE

ARROW ROAD

NEXT RIGHT

PUTTING WORDS IN THEIR PLACE

Fill in the blanks.

Use the words in the list.

> point
> top
> clues
> way
> list

1. You can use ——————— to find the main ——————— of

   a ———————.

2. The words at the ——————— of a list can give you a clue.

3. The ——————— the list is used can give you a clue.

LOOKING AT WORDS

Fill in the blanks.

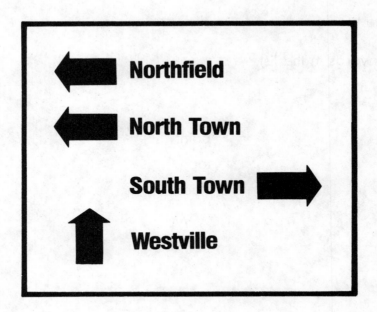

This is a l__st of towns.

The l__st is on a road s__gn.

Th__re is no heading on the l__st.

But you can t__ll the m____n p____nt of the l__st.

The way the l__st is used g__ves you a clue about the

m____n p____nt.

TRYING IT ON YOUR OWN

Look for lists.

Does the list have a heading?

Does the heading give the main point of the list?

Can you find other clues to the main point?

UNIT 11

A list is one way to put things in order.

A list can make something easier to read.

It can make something easier to understand.

You can use clues to find things in a list.

Look at this list.

TV SHOWS

7:00 PM

2 **News**
4 **News**
6 **Good Buys**—with
   Al Jones
8 **News**
10 **Life at Home**—Comedy

7:30 PM

2 **TV Today**—Talk Show
4 **Something to Say**—Talk Show
8 **Movie:** Don't Answer the
   Telephone—with Rex North
   and Jane Blanks
10 **Fish Eggs**—Comedy

What is this list for?

This is part of a list of TV shows.

The list tells you what is on TV.

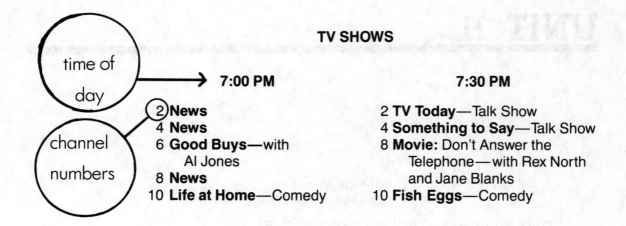

TV SHOWS

time of day

channel numbers

7:00 PM

② **News**
4 **News**
6 **Good Buys**—with Al Jones
8 **News**
10 **Life at Home**—Comedy

7:30 PM

2 **TV Today**—Talk Show
4 **Something to Say**—Talk Show
8 **Movie:** Don't Answer the Telephone—with Rex North and Jane Blanks
10 **Fish Eggs**—Comedy

Look at how the list of TV shows is put together.

Look at the parts of the list.

The number above each group in the list tells you the time of day.

The shows listed under the time of day start at that time.

Now look at the numbers next to the shows.

These numbers tell you what channels the shows are on.

―――――――――

You know what the list is for.

You know how the parts are put together.

This makes it easier to find out what shows are on TV.

All you do is find the time of day.

Then look at the shows listed under that time.

Can you answer these questions about the TV list?

1. What show is on channel 4 at 7:30 PM?

2. What show is on channel 2 at 7:00 PM?

3. What time does the movie on channel 8 start?

4. Look at the shows listed under 7:30 PM. On what channel is the show "Fish Eggs"?

5. Does the list make it easy for you to find the shows?

Here is another list.

North Town Food Store

Our prices are the lowest in town!

Now on sale:

"Java" coffee . . . . **$ 2.99/can**

Eggs (grade A large) **$1.09/dozen**

Milk . . . . **$ .79/quart**

"YES" soap . . . . **3 for $1.09**

Other stores can't match our prices!

North Town Food Store
1309 Ridge Road.
(at the North Town Mall)

This is an ad.

It has a list in it.

What is the list for?

The list shows the prices of things on sale.

How are the parts of the list put together?

The things on sale are listed at the left.

The prices are listed on the right.

Can you answer these questions about the list?

1. How much is a quart of milk at the store?

2. How much is a can of "Java" coffee?

3. What is the sale price of a dozen eggs?

4. Does the list make it easy for you to find the prices?

A list is one way to put things in order.

A list can make something easier to read.

It can make something easier to understand.

You can use these clues to read a list.

1. Find out what the list is for.

2. Look at the parts of the list.

3. Look at how the parts are put together.

These clues can make a list easier to read and understand.

TRYING IT OUT

Look at each list.

Then answer the questions about it.

9:00 PM

  2   THE GOOD GUYS—Comedy
  4   MOVIE: KILLER BUGS
       —with Jay Price
  6   BASEBALL
  8   THE ED LEACH SHOW—Music
10   NEWARK—Drama

9:30 PM

  2   IT CAN'T ADD UP!—Comedy
  8   FIND YOUR LIFE—Talk Show
10   LOOKING FOR ANSWERS—Drama

1.   What is this list for?

2.   What show is on channel 8 at 9:00 PM?

3.   What show is on channel 10 at 9:30 PM?

4.   What time does the movie on channel 4 start?

Let us drive you there.

Riley Cab Company

Rates (From North Town)

To South Town	$3.50
To North Point	$3.75
To Westville	$4.50
To Goodland	$5.00

1. What does the list show?

2. How much is it to go from North Town to South Town?

3. How much is it to go from North Town to Westville?

4. How much is it to go from North Town to Goodland?

PUTTING WORDS IN THEIR PLACE

Fill in the blanks.

Use the words in the list.

North Town Food Store

Our prices are the lowest in town!

<u>Now on sale:</u>

"Java" coffee . . . . $ 2.99/can

Eggs (grade A large) $1.09/dozen

Milk . . . . $ .79/quart

"YES" soap . . . . 3 for $1.09

Other stores can't match our prices!

North Town Food Store

1309 Ridge Road.

(at the North Town Mall)

---

prices

right

food

list

sale

1. This is an ad for a ——————— store.

2. The ad has a ——————— in it.

3. The list shows the ——————— of things on ———————.

4. The prices are listed on the ———————.

TRYING IT ON YOUR OWN

Look for a list of TV shows.

What are the parts of the list?

How are the parts put together?

Does the list make it easy for you to find a show?

LOOKING AT WORDS

Fill in the blanks.

A l__st is one w__y to put th__ngs in ord__r.

A l__st c__n make s__meth__ng easier to read.

It c__n make s__meth__ng easier to und__rst__nd.

You c__n use these clues to r____d a list:

1. F__nd out wh__t the l__st is for.

2. L____k at the th__ngs in the l__st.

3. L____k at h__w the th__ngs are put t__geth__r.

UNIT 12   (REVIEW)

Look at the sign.

Then answer the questions about it.

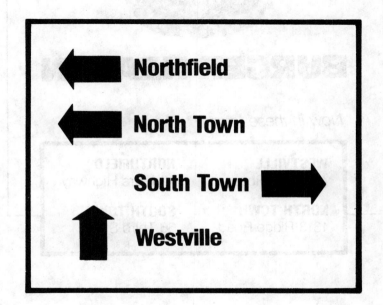

1. What is the sign for?

2. What things are listed on the sign?

3. What do the arrows tell you?

4. You are driving on the road.

    You want to go to Westville.

    You get to this sign.

    How do you get to Westville from this point?

Look at the ad.

Then answer the questions about it.

1. What is the ad for?

2. What is listed in the ad?

3. Why is the list in the ad?

4. You want to go to a "Burger Heaven."

   You are in South Town.

   Where do you go to get to the "Burger Heaven"?

Fill in the blanks.

Use the words in the list.

MIKE'S COFFEE SHOP

Price list for drinks:

Coffee	50¢
Tea	45¢
Milk	65¢
Soda	75¢
Beer	$1.00

Add 10¢ for orders "to go"

---

coffee

cup

list

price

soda

drinks

This is a price ——————.

The list tells you the prices of —————— at "Mike's

—————— Shop."

A —————— is 75¢ at "Mike's."

A —————— of coffee is 50¢.

You add 10¢ to the —————— if the order is "to go."

Fill in the blanks.

TV SHOWS

7:00 PM	7:30 PM
2 **News**	2 **TV Today**—Talk Show
4 **News**	4 **Something to Say**—Talk Show
6 **Good Buys**—with Al Jones	8 **Movie:** Don't Answer the Telephone—with Rex North and Jane Blanks
8 **News**	
10 **Life at Home**—Comedy	10 **Fish Eggs**—Comedy

This is part of a l__st of TV sh__ws.

The top n__mbers in the l__st t__ll' you the time of d__y.

The n__mbers on the left are the ch__nn__l n__mbers.

You c__n use the l__st to f__nd out what t__me a

TV sh__w starts.

You c__n use the l__st to f__nd out what ch__nn__l a

TV sh__w is on.

82

UNIT 13

Think about this.

You want to go out to eat.

You pick a place to go.

The place may have a list of foods you can order.

The list shows the prices of the foods.

The list is a <u>menu</u>.

A menu tells you what kind of foods a place has.

It also tells you the prices of the foods.

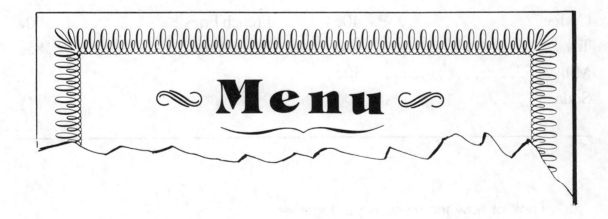

Here is part of a menu.

KATE'S DINER

Open 24 hours a day

EGGS
(served all day)

2 eggs (any style)	95¢
with Ham	$1.65
with Bacon	$1.65
with Sausage	$1.75

BURGERS

Plain Burger	$1.95
Cheeseburger	$2.25
Cheeseburger with Bacon	$2.40

DRINKS

Coffee	40¢
Tea	40¢
Milk	50¢
Soda	60¢

SIDE ORDERS

French Fries	90¢
Home Fries	85¢

Look at how the menu is put together.

The foods are listed under headings.

The prices are listed to the right of the foods.

You go to "Kate's Diner."

You want a cheeseburger and a soda.

How would you use the menu?

You could use it to find out the prices of what you want.

Find the heading for burgers.

Look at the list under the heading.

Can you find the price of a cheeseburger?

The price is $2.25.

Now look under the heading for drinks.

How much is a soda?

The menu tells you that a soda is 60¢.

You can use a menu to find the price of something you want.

But sometimes you don't know what you want.

How would you use a menu then?

You could use it to pick out something to eat.

The menu could give you an idea of what to eat.

You could look at the headings on the menu.

Then you could look at the lists under the headings for other
    ideas.

You may not know all the things on a menu.

But you can use clues to find out what the things are.

Look at this list from a menu.

EGGS

2 eggs . . . . 95¢
    with Ham $1.65
    with Bacon $1.65
    with Sausage $1.75
Omelette $1.25
    with Cheese $1.75

You may not know the word "omelette."

But can you guess what an omelette is made of?

The word "omelette" is listed under the heading "Eggs."

You can guess that an omelette is made with eggs.

The heading gives you this clue.

You may not know what a heading means.

But you can use clues to find out.

Look at this list.

POULTRY

Fried Chicken $4.25
Baked Chicken $4.95
Chicken Sandwich. $3.50
Roast Turkey $4.95
Roast Duck $5.95

You may not know the word "Poultry."

But you know that it's a heading.

It's at the top of the list.

The things in the list must be kinds of poultry.

What are the things listed?

The things listed are chicken, turkey, and duck.

You can guess that "Poultry" stands for chicken, turkey, and duck.

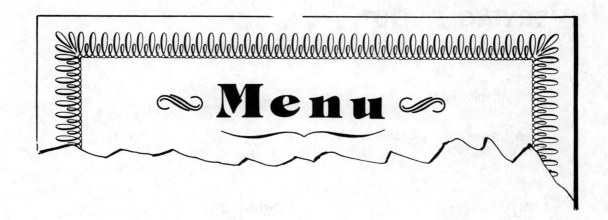

A menu is a list.

You may use a menu when you go out to eat.

A menu lists the foods that a place has.

It also lists the prices of the foods.

You could use a menu to find the price of something.

You could use a menu to get an idea if you don't know what you want.

You may not know all the things on a menu.

But you can use clues to guess what the things are.

TRYING IT OUT

Look at this menu.

Then answer the questions about it.

Soup

Chicken $1.00
Pea $1.00
Minestrone $1.00

Salad

Plain $1.50
Chef's $4.50

Beef

Hamburger $2.50
Cheeseburger $2.85
Roast Beef Sandwich. $3.95
Steak Sandwich $4.25

Poultry

Chicken Salad Sandwich. $2.50
Fried Chicken $4.25
House Special $4.25

Fish

Fish Sandwich. $2.75
Fried Fish $4.50
Flounder $4.75
Halibut $4.95

Dessert

Ice Cream $1.00
Cheesecake $1.75
Pie of the day $1.75

Drinks

Coffee . . . . $.50
Tea. . . . . $.50
Soda . . . . $.75

1. How much is a chef's salad?

2. How much is a fish sandwich?

3. What kind of food is "minestrone"? How can you tell?

4. What kind of food is "halibut"? What clue tells you this?

5. Can you tell what kind of food is in the "House Special"?

PUTTING WORDS IN THEIR PLACE

Fill in the blanks.

Use one of the words under the blank.

Example: A menu _____is_____ a list.

does
is
has

A menu tells you _____ kinds of foods a _____ has.

what   menu
where   place
why   price

A menu also _____ you the price of _____ foods.

lists   that
says   the
tells   this

You could use _____ menu to find the _____ of something.

a   menu
and   place
but   price

LOOKING AT WORDS

Some long words are made up of two short words put together.

Some of these words are used below.

Find them.

Show the two short words that make up the long word.

Example: (Some|times) you may use a menu.

1. They like to eat cheeseburgers.

2. You can order coffee and cheesecake.

3. I would like a cupcake for dessert.

4. You can use a menu to pick out something to eat.

5. The menu does not list beefsteak.

TRYING IT ON YOUR OWN

Look at a menu.

Look for things that you don't know.

Can you use clues to find out what the things are?

UNIT 14

A menu is a list of things to eat.

A menu also shows the prices of things to eat.

Here is another list.

This list is on a road sign.

Look at the sign.

Then answer the questions about it.

North Town	3
Westville	5
South Town	8

What is listed on the sign?

What do the numbers mean?

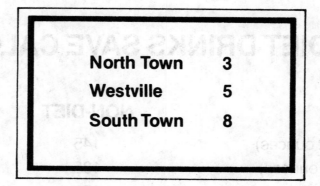

North Town	3
Westville	5
South Town	8

There is a list of towns on the sign.

The numbers next to the towns stand for miles.

The sign tells you North Town is three miles away.

This sign is easy to understand if you know what the numbers
   stand for.

How many miles is it to Westville?

How many miles is it to South Town?

Here is another list.

The list has numbers in it.

Look at how the list is put together.

Then answer the questions about it.

HOW DIET DRINKS SAVE CALORIES

	NON-DIET	DIET
Soda (12 ounces)	145	1
Beer (12 ounces)	135	95
Milk (1 cup)	150	85 (skim)
Fruit Punch (10 ounces)	130	20

What are the things in the list?

What is the main point of the list?

What do the numbers stand for?

How can you tell?

Look at how the list is put together.

The heading tells you the main point.

The main point is to show how diet drinks save calories.

The drinks are listed at the left.

The numbers are at the right.

There are headings above the numbers.

The headings tell you what the numbers stand for.

The numbers under the heading "NON-DIET" show one thing.

They show the number of calories in non-diet drinks.

The numbers under "DIET" show another thing.

They show the number of calories in diet drinks.

How would you find something in the list?

You can use these three clues to find something in the list:

1. You know the main point of the list.

2. You know what the parts of the list are.

3. You know how the list is put together.

These three clues can help you find something in the list.

The clues can help you to answer questions about the list.

Look at the question at the top of the next page.

Look at how the clues are used to answer the question.

How many calories are in 10 ounces of diet fruit punch?

HOW DIET DRINKS SAVE CALORIES

	NON-DIET	DIET	2. Find list for diet drinks
Soda (12 ounces)	145	1	
Beer (12 ounces)	135	95	
Milk (1 cup)	150	85 (skim)	
1. Find drink → Fruit Punch (10 ounces)	130	20 ←	3. Find number

How would you answer this question?

You know the parts of the list.

You know that the drinks are listed at the left.

Look for "Fruit Punch" at the left in the list.

"Fruit Punch" is the last line in the list.

You know that the numbers stand for calories.

The question asks about diet fruit punch.

Look for the heading '"DIET."

Go down the list of numbers until you get to the line for fruit punch.

The number is "20."

There are 20 calories in 10 ounces of diet fruit punch.

Some lists are long.

They have many parts.

They look hard to read.

But finding things in a long list can be easy.

It can be easy if you use the clues.

Look at this list.

What's in the food you eat?

FOOD	Size of Serving	Calories	Grams of protein	Grams of fat
Burger	3 ounces	185	23	10
Chicken	3 ounces	120	21	3
Eggs	3 ounces	130	8	9
Fish	3 ounces	135	22	4
Ham	3 ounces	245	18	19
Roast Beef	3 ounces	165	25	7

Clue 1:   Find the main point of the list.

The heading of the list gives you a clue about the main point.

The heading is a question.

The question is: "What's in the food you eat?"

The list answers the question.

The main point is to tell you what some foods have in them.

Clue 2:   Look at what the parts of the list are.

This is a list of foods.

The list has numbers in it.

It has headings.

The headings tell you what the numbers mean.

Clue 3:   Look at how the list is put together.

The foods are listed at the left.

The numbers at the right tell you things about the foods.

Use the clues to answer the questions about the list.

What's in the food you eat?

FOOD	Size of Serving	Calories	Grams of protein	Grams of fat
Burger	3 ounces	185	23	10
Chicken	3 ounces	120	21	3
Eggs	3 ounces	130	8	9
Fish	3 ounces	135	22	4
Ham	3 ounces	245	18	19
Roast Beef	3 ounces	165	25	7

1. How many calories are in 3 ounces of chicken?

2. How many grams of fat are in 3 ounces of roast beef?

3. How many grams of protein are in 3 ounces of fish?

4. Look at all the foods in the list.
   What food has the most calories in it?

5. What food in the list has the most grams of fat in it?

6. What food in the list has the most grams of protein in it?

TRYING IT OUT

Look at this ad.

Then answer the questions about it.

Art's TV Heaven

Price List

12-inch black & white TV	$ 79
19-inch black & white TV	$149
21-inch black & white TV	$199
12-inch color TV	$199
19-inch color TV	$349
21-inch color TV	$429
25-inch color TV	$549

You can't beat our prices!

1. What is this ad for?

2. What does the list tell you?

3. What is the price of a 19-inch color TV?

4. What is the price of a 12-inch black & white TV?

5. Look at all the TV's in the list.
   What two TV's have the same price?

PUTTING WORDS IN THEIR PLACE

Fill in the blanks.

Use one of the words under the blank.

Some lists look hard _____ read.

                and
                for
                to

But you can _____ clues to find things _____ a long list.

      look   at
      use   in
      you   it

Here _____ the clues.

      also
      are
      or

1. Find the _____ point of the list.

        made
        main
        makes

2. _____ at what the parts _____ the list are.

     Here   of
     Look   or
     There   up

3. Look _____ how the list is _____ together.

      at   part
      out   put
      up   up

LOOKING AT WORDS

You looked at these two words on page 96.

diet   non-diet

The word "diet" is in each word.

But the words don't mean the same thing.

The second word starts with "non."

"Non" means "not."

The second word means "not diet."

Here are some more words that start with "non."

What do they mean?

1. Skim milk is a <u>non-fat</u> drink.

2. The bus ride from North Town to South Town is <u>nonstop</u>.

3. The store also sells <u>nonfood</u> things.

TRYING IT ON YOUR OWN

Look for lists that have numbers in them.

Do the lists have headings?

Do the headings make the lists easier to read?

UNIT 15

Here is another kind of list.

Look at it.

Then answer the questions about it.

ARROW BUS COMPANY TIMETABLE
Bus Number 102   from South Town
to North Town

LEAVES SOUTH TOWN:	WESTVILLE Main Street	WESTVILLE East Road	NORTHFIELD Oak Street	NORTHFIELD Mars Highway	NORTH TOWN Park Avenue	NORTH TOWN Ridge Road
10:00AM	10:10AM	10:25AM	10:35AM	10:43AM	10:51AM	11:02AM
11:30AM	11:40AM	11:55AM	12:05PM	12:13PM	12:21PM	12:32PM
1:00PM	1:10PM	1:25PM	1:35PM	1:43PM	1:51PM	2:02PM
2:30PM	2:40PM	2:55PM	3:05PM	3:13PM	3:21PM	3:32PM
4:00PM	4:10PM	4:25PM	4:35PM	4:43PM	4:51PM	5:02PM
6:00PM	6:10PM	6:25PM	6:35PM	6:43PM	6:51PM	7:02PM
8:30PM	8:40PM	8:55PM	9:05PM	9:13PM	9:21PM	9:32PM

What is this list for?

What are the parts of the list?

How are the parts put together?

106

The list is a <u>timetable</u>.

A timetable is a kind of list.

A timetable shows when something is supposed to happen.

The timetable on the last page is for a bus.

The bus goes from South Town to North Town.

The headings on the timetable are the names of places.

The bus stops at these places.

The numbers in the timetable show times of day.

The numbers show the time the bus is supposed to get to each
place.

ARROW BUS COMPANY TIMETABLE

Bus Number 102   from South Town
to North Town

LEAVES SOUTH TOWN:	WESTVILLE Main Street	WESTVILLE East Road	NORTHFIELD Oak Street	NORTHFIELD Mars Highway	NORTH TOWN Park Avenue	NORTH TOWN Ridge Road ①.
10:00AM	10:10AM	10:25AM	10:35AM	10:43AM	10:51AM	11:02AM
11:30AM	11:40AM	11:55AM	12:05PM	12:13PM	12:21PM	12:32PM
③. 1:00PM	1:10PM	1:25PM	1:35PM	1:43PM	1:51PM	2:02PM ②.
2:30PM	2:40PM	2:55PM	3:05PM	3:13PM	3:21PM	3:32PM
4:00PM	4:10PM	4:25PM	4:35PM	4:43PM	4:51PM	5:02PM
6:00PM	6:10PM	6:25PM	6:35PM	6:43PM	6:51PM	7:02PM
8:30PM	8:40PM	8:55PM	9:05PM	9:13PM	9:21PM	9:32PM

You can use a timetable to find out when to get the bus.

Here is an example.

You are in South Town.

You want to go to Ridge Road in North Town.

You want to get there at about 2:30 PM.

What time should you get the bus?

Here's how to find out:

1. Find the heading for Ridge Road in North Town.

   It's the last heading on the timetable.

2. Go down the list of times under that heading.

   Find the time that is closest to 2:30 PM.

   The closest time is 2:02 PM.

3. Go across the 2:02 PM line.

   Find the time that the bus leaves South Town.

   The time the bus leaves is at the left.

   The bus leaves at 1:00 PM.

You should get the 1:00 PM bus to get to Ridge Road in North
   Town at about 2:30 PM.

Finding something in a timetable often is easy.

You don't have to read the whole timetable.

All you have to do is use the clues for reading a list.

1.   Find the main point.

2.   Look at the parts of the timetable.

3.   Look at how the parts are put together.

Then use the clues to find what you want to know.

ARROW BUS COMPANY TIMETABLE

Bus Number 102   from South Town
                                  to North Town

LEAVES SOUTH TOWN:	WESTVILLE Main Street	WESTVILLE East Road	NORTHFIELD Oak Street	NORTHFIELD Mars Highway	NORTH TOWN Park Avenue	NORTH TOWN Ridge Road
10:00AM	10:10AM	10:25AM	10:35AM	10:43AM	10:51AM	11:02AM
11:30AM	11:40AM	11:55AM	12:05PM	12:13PM	12:21PM	12:32PM
1:00PM	1:10PM	1:25PM	1:35PM	1:43PM	1:51PM	2:02PM
2:30PM	2:40PM	2:55PM	3:05PM	3:13PM	3:21PM	3:32PM
4:00PM	4:10PM	4:25PM	4:35PM	4:43PM	4:51PM	5:02PM
6:00PM	6:10PM	6:25PM	6:35PM	6:43PM	6:51PM	7:02PM
8:30PM	8:40PM	8:55PM	9:05PM	9:13PM	9:21PM	9:32PM

TRYING IT OUT

Use the clues to answer the questions about the timetable.

1. You get on the bus in South Town at 2:30 PM.

    What time should you get to Oak Street in Northfield?

2. You are in South Town.

    You want to go to East Road in Westville.

    You want to get there at about 3:00 PM.

    What time should you get the bus in South Town?

3. You are at Mars Highway in Northfield.

    You want to go to Ridge Road in North Town.

    You want to get there at about 5:00 PM.

    What time should you get the bus?

4. The time is 1:15 PM.

    You are at the Oak Street bus stop in Northfield.

    You want to get the bus to North Town.

    When is the next bus to North Town?

PUTTING WORDS IN THEIR PLACE

Fill in the blanks.

Use one of the words under the blank.

You can use _____ clues to find something
                 here
                 that
                 these

_____ a timetable.
    in
    of
    to

1. Find the _____ point.
              kind
              main
              mile

2. Look at the _____ of the timetable.
                parts
                place
                time

3. Look _____ how the parts are _____ together.
       at   page
       in   place
       out   put

LOOKING AT WORDS

Here are two things from the timetable.

          10:00 AM   1:00 PM

"AM" is short for "before noon."

"PM" is short for "after noon."

Some of the words below are short for other words.

Can you tell what the short words mean?

The timetable is from the Arrow Bus <u>Co.</u>

The timetable is for Bus <u>No.</u> 102.

The bus stop at Main <u>St.</u> in Westville.

It stops at East <u>Rd.</u> in Westville.

It stops at Mars <u>Hwy.</u> in Northfield.

It also stops at Park <u>Ave.</u> in North Town.

TRYING IT ON YOUR OWN

Get a timetable for a bus or a train.

Do the clues help you to find things in the timetable?

UNIT 16   (REVIEW)

Look at this list.

Then answer the questions about it on the next page.

RITA'S HOUSE OF FOOD

——open 24 hrs. a day——
——open 7 days a week——

TODAY'S LUNCH SPECIALS

Soup of the Day
Pea Soup $1.25

Burgers
Plain Burger $1.95
Cheeseburger. $2.25
Bacon Burger $2.45
Rita's Special $2.95

Sandwiches
Chicken Salad. $2.75
Ham Salad $2.95
Egg Salad $2.95
Fried Fish $3.50
Roast Beef. $3.75
Steak $3.95
Cheesesteak. $4.50

Look at our everyday menu
for our complete food list.

1. What is the name of the diner?

2. The second line on the menu says "open 24 hrs. a day."

   What does "hrs." stand for?

3. Look for "Rita's Special" in the list of foods.

   What is the main thing in "Rita's Special"?

   How can you tell?

4. How much is a cheesesteak sandwich?

5. How much is a bacon burger?

6. Does this list show you all the foods you can get at the
   diner?

Here's a list of TV shows.

Look at it.

Then answer the questions about it on the next page.

TV TODAY

6:00 PM

(3)–NEWS
(5)–NEWS
(7)–THE $20,000 GIVEAWAY
   —Game Show

6:30 PM

(7)–THE BIG BEAT—Music
(9)–GOOD IDEAS—Talk Show

7:00 PM

(3)–ALL ABOUT FOOD
   —with Chef Leon
(5)–THE SECOND PAGE
   —News Show
(7)–HERE'S TO YOU—Talk Show
(9)–THERE GOES MOE—Comedy

7:30 PM

(3)–NEW IDEAS—Talk Show
(7)–IT'S YOUR TURN—Comedy
(9)–BASEBALL

8:00 PM

(3)–HOW'S THAT!—Comedy
(5)–COPS—Drama
(7)–MOVIE: THE LAST HOUSE
   ON THE RIGHT—Drama

8:30 PM

(3)–THE KEN JONES SHOW
   —Comedy

9:00 PM

(3)–MOVIE: MILES OF HIGHWAY
   —Drama
(5)–RIDE THE TRAIN
   —Comedy/Drama

9:30 PM

(9)–YOU AND YOUR LUNCH
   —with Dr. Elsa Sizemore

10:00 PM

(5)–NEWS
(7)–NEWS
(9)–THE MARIA LOPEZ SHOW
   —Music

1. What are the parts of this list?

2. How are the parts put together?

3. What show on channel 7 starts at 6:30 PM?

4. What show on channel 3 starts at 7:30 PM?

5. "The Second Page" is on channel 5 at 7:00 PM.

   What kind of show is "The Second Page"?

   How can you tell?

6. Look at the shows that start at 7:00 PM.

   What channel has a talk show on at 7:00 PM?

7. How many movies are listed?

   What times do they start?

   What channels are they on?

8. Could you use this list to find out how long a show is?

   How could you do it?

Look at this timetable.

Then answer the questions about it.

ARROW BUS COMPANY TIMETABLE
Bus Number 30   from Northfield
to South Town

LEAVES NORTHFIELD:	NORTH TOWN Main St.	NORTH TOWN Second St.	WESTVILLE Belt Hwy.	WESTVILLE White Ave.	WESTVILLE Third Ave.	SOUTH TOWN South Rd.
10:00AM	10:15AM	10:32AM	11:03AM	11:14AM	11:26AM	11:47AM
(X) 12:30PM	12:45PM	1:02PM	———	———	———	1:52PM
2:00PM	2:15PM	2:32PM	3:03PM	3:14PM	3:26PM	3:47PM
3:30PM	3:45PM	4:02PM	4:33PM	4:44PM	4:56PM	5:17PM
(X) 5:00PM	5:15PM	5:32PM	———	———	———	6:22PM
6:30PM	6:45PM	7:02PM	7:33PM	7:44PM	7:56PM	8:17PM
(X) 8:00PM	8:15PM	8:32PM	———	———	———	9:22PM

(X) — Express Bus

1. You get on the bus in Northfield at 6:30 PM.

   What time should you get to South Town?

2. You are in Northfield.

   You want to go to White Ave. in Westville.

   You want to get there at about 3:30 PM.

   What time should you get the bus in Northfield?

3. Look at the timetable for the 12:30 PM bus from Northfield.

   Why are some of the spaces left blank?

118

Here are some lines about the timetable on page 118.

Fill in the blanks.

Use one of the words under the blank.

This is a timetable _____ the Arrow Bus Company.

        at
        from
        to

_____ is for Bus No. 30.

   Here
   It
   The

_____ No. 30 goes from Northfield _____ South Town.

Arrow   at
Belt   from
Bus   to

The names at _____ top tell you the _____ where the bus stops.

     the   pictures
     this   places
     to   times

_____ times at the left _____ you when the bus

   Tell   tell
   The   this
   This   to

_____ Northfield.

    gets
    leaves
    lines

The last stop _____ at South Road in _____ .

       in   Northfield
       is   North Town
       it   South Town

Look at the underlined words.

Tell what each underlined word means.

Peg rides the No. 30 bus each day.

She gets on the bus at Second St. in North Town.

She takes the bus to South Rd. in South Town.

She likes to get the bus at 1:02 PM.

The 1:02 PM bus goes nonstop to South Town.

_____

Bert goes to Kate's Diner for lunch each day.

He eats the same things each day.

He has three cheeseburgers.

He also has a large order of French fries.

He has some cheesecake for dessert.

He drinks non-fat milk with his lunch.

UNIT 17

Think about this.

You go to a diner.

You look at the menu.

You want to find out the price of a cup of coffee.

Where would you look?

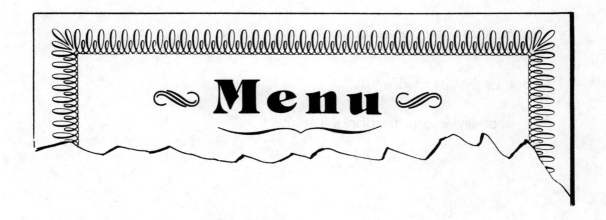

Drinks

Coffee . . . . 50¢

Tea . . . . 50¢

Milk . . . . 60¢

Soda . . . . 75¢

You would look for a heading.

The heading tells you what is listed under it.

You could guess that "coffee" would be listed under "Drinks."

Headings are one way to put things in order.

Headings tell what the things in a list are.

But how are the names in the list put in order?

Look at the list of drinks.

In what order are the drinks listed?

The drinks are listed in price order.

The drinks that cost the least are listed first.

The drinks that cost the most are listed last.

Coffee and tea cost only 50¢.

They are listed first.

Soda costs 75¢.

It is listed last.

Price order is only one way to put things in order.

Here is another way.

Can you tell what it is?

Coffee
Milk
Soda
Tea

<u>C</u>offee

<u>M</u>ilk

<u>S</u>oda

<u>T</u>ea

The four words are in <u>alphabetical</u> order.

What does "alphabetical order" mean?

Look at the first letter in each word.

Now think about the letters in the alphabet.

A B <u>C</u> D E F G H I J K L <u>M</u> N O P Q R <u>S</u> <u>T</u> U V W X Y Z

The letter <u>C</u> comes before <u>M</u>, <u>S</u>, or <u>T</u> in the alphabet.

"Coffee" starts with a <u>C</u>.

"Coffee" is listed first.

"Milk" is listed second.

"Soda" is listed third.

"Tea" is listed last.

Here's a list with more words:

Beer
Coffee
Juice
Soda
Tea

Look at where the new words are put.

The letter B comes before C in the alphabet.

"Beer" is put before "Coffee" in the list.

The letter J comes before M but after C.

"Juice" is put between "Coffee" and "Milk" in the list.

<u>B</u>eer

<u>C</u>offee

<u>J</u>uice

<u>M</u>ilk

<u>S</u>oda

<u>T</u>ea

There are many ways to put words in order.

One way is to use alphabetical order.

Look at the first letter of each word.

Then think about the order of the alphabet.

The alphabet tells you where the word should be in the list.

A B C D E F G H I J K L M N O P Q R S T U V W X Y Z

TRYING IT OUT

Look at each list.

What kind of order is used in the list?

What's in the food you eat?

FOOD	Size of Serving	Calories	Grams of protein	Grams of fat
Burger	3 ounces	185	23	10
Chicken	3 ounces	120	21	3
Eggs	3 ounces	130	8	9
Fish	3 ounces	135	22	4
Ham	3 ounces	245	18	19
Roast Beef	3 ounces	165	25	7

North Town	**3**
Westville	**5**
South Town	**8**

Beef

Hamburger $2.50
Cheeseburger $2.85
Roast Beef Sandwich $3.95
Steak Sandwich $4.25

PUTTING WORDS IN THEIR PLACE

Fill in the blanks.

Use one of the words under the blank.

Beer

Coffee

Juice

Milk

Soda

Tea

This list is in _____ order.

        alphabetical
        another
        price

Look at the _____ letter of each word.

        first
        last
        order

_____ letters are in the _____ order as they are

It   list
The   same
This   size

_____ the alphabet.

        at
        in
        of

The alphabet _____ you where each word _____ be in the list.

        says   should
        tells   show
        times   starts

LOOKING AT WORDS

You looked at these two words on page 124.

<u>alphabet</u>   <u>alphabetical</u>

The two words are almost the same.

The second word has "alphabet" in it.

But it has another part added to it.

Look at each <u>underlined</u> word below.

Do you know any of the parts in the word?

Can you tell what the word means?

———————————

Here are some words to think about.

Question things that are <u>questionable</u>.

Understand things that are <u>understandable</u>.

Find meaning in things that are <u>meaningful</u>.

TRYING IT ON YOUR OWN

Can you think of any lists that are in alphabetical order?

Does the order make the list easier to use?

UNIT 18

When is alphabetical order used?

Here is one example.

It is a list of offices in the North Town City Hall.

OFFICE   FLOOR

Civil Court	2
Deeds & Records	1
Fire Chief	2
Health Dept.	3
Police Dept.	1
Recreation & Parks Dept.	2
Social Services	1
Traffic Court	3

The order makes it easier to find something.

It can save you time if you are looking for something.

You don't have to read all the names in the list.

All you do is look down the list for the right letter.

Suppose you want to find the Police Department.

How would you do this?

OFFICE   FLOOR

Office	Floor
Civil Court	2
Deeds & Records	1
Fire Chief	2
Health Dept.	3
Police Dept.	①
Recreation & Parks Dept.	2
Social Services	1
Traffic Court	3

P is the first letter in "Police."

Look down the list for the letter P.

You will find the listing for the Police Department.

The number across from "Police Dept." tells you the floor.

A phone book is a kind of list.

The names in a phone book are in alphabetical order.

Here is a list of names from a phone book.

Lake V	19 Oak St.	513-7229
Leach E	23 Ridge Rd.	712-5638
LINCOLN FOOD SHOP		
	246 Mars Hwy.	712-3678
Lloyd C	342 Oak St.	513-4787
Lopez H	46 Third St.	812-9989
Lucas J	3 First St.	712-4882

All of the names start with <u>L</u>.

But the names are in alphabetical order.

Can you tell how the names are put in order?

Look at the second letter in each name.

The second letter is used to put the names in order.

What if the second letters are the same?

Then the third letters are used.

Lucas J	3 First St.	712-4882
Ludlum P	32 First St.	712-3372
Lum T	486 Oak St.	513-0091
Lund J	59 Third St.	812-7205
Lutz R	324 Ridge Rd.	712-5810

Alphabetical order can make a list easier to use.

You don't have to read the whole list to find something.

You can find something by looking for letters.

TRYING IT OUT

Here is a list from a phone book.

Answer the questions about it.

Find the answers by using alphabetical order.

MACK'S DINER
    872 Main St Westville   218-8100
Martin K   22 First St NrthTwn   913-7253
Matthews T   14 Day Rd SthTwn   712-5211
Maxwell J   171 12th St SthTwn   712-3261
Meeker K   19 Ridge Rd NrthTwn   812-5721
MEN'S WORLD STORE
    46 Mars Hwy South Town   217-2210
Mertz F   212 Day Rd SthTwn   712-8779
MEXICO TRAVEL AGENCY
    22 Ridge Rd North Town   511-1212
Miller A   468 Black Ave Wstville   218-7672
Miller Z   26 Main St Wstville   706-2358
Milner K   282 Ridge Rd NrthTwn   812-9601
Milton J   46 8th St SthTwn   217-7600
Minor C   362 Main St Wstville   706-7201
Minow F   488 First St NrthTwn   913-3821
Minowski J   96 Day Rd SthTwn   712-1365

1. What is the phone number of F. Mertz?

2. What is the phone number of Men's World Store?

3. What is the phone number of K. Milner?

4. On what street does C. Minor live?

5. On what street does K. Meeker live?

6. Can you tell what <u>NrthTwn</u>, <u>SthTwn</u>, and <u>Wstville</u> stand for?

   How can you tell?

7. There are two listings for the name <u>Miller</u>.

   Why do you think A. Miller is listed before Z. Miller?

PUTTING WORDS IN THEIR PLACE

Fill in the blanks.

Use one of the words under the blank.

A long list can ——————— hard to use.

                are
                be
                is

Alphabetical ——————— makes it easier to ——————— a long list.

             list   find
             order   save
             other   use

It ——————— it easier to find ——————— in a long list.

     makes   listing
     means   looking
     names   something

——————— don't have to read ——————— the names in the ———————.

   This   all   floor
   Use   each   list
   You   easy   street

You can find something ——————— looking for the letters.

                  at
                  but
                  by

LOOKING AT WORDS

You have looked at some lists from a phone book.

Some of the words in the lists are short for other words.

"Rd." is short for "Road."

"St." is short for "Street."

Read the lines below.

Look at the underlined words.

They are short for other words.

Can you guess what words they are short for?

1. What is the largest city in the U.S.?

2. You should bake the cake for 2 hrs.

3. You are on pg. 137 of this book.

4. There is a new TV show on Ch. 2.

TRYING IT ON YOUR OWN

Look at the want ads in a newspaper.

Are the ads in alphabetical order?

Look at the words in the ads.

Are some of the words short for other words?

Can you guess what they mean?

UNIT 19 (REVIEW)

You have looked at a lot of things in this book.

You have looked at signs.

You've looked at ads.

You've looked at lists.

You have also looked at some clues.

The clues can make things easier to read.

They can make things easier to understand.

There are some things to read on the next pages.

There are questions about them.

Answer the questions.

Use the clues you have looked at.

Here are two signs.

1. What does the first sign tell you?

2. What does the second sign tell you?

3. What does the list on the second sign mean?

4. Look at the first sign.

   Do the words and the pictures say the same thing?

5. Where do you think you would find these signs?

Here is a sign.

1. What is "Jack's Roadhouse"?

2. How can you tell?

3. What does the sign say?

4. Look at the word "Roadhouse."

    It is made up of two short words.

    What are the two words?

5. Look at the last line in the sign.

    What does "hrs." mean?

Here is an ad.

There is only one good reason to drive safely.

It can save your life.

1. What is this ad about?

2. What does the ad say?

3. Why do you think the ad is used?

4. What does the picture show?

5. How does the picture help you to get the main point?

Here is an ad.

1. What is the ad for?

2. Look at the list in the ad.

    Why is the list used?

3. Look at the underlined words in the list.

    What do they tell you?

4. Look for "The Chef's Special" in the list.

    Can you guess what is in "The Chef's Special"?

    Does the ad give you a clue?

5. Look at the word "Fowl."

    Can you guess what "Fowl" stands for?

    Does the ad give you a clue?

6. Look at the things listed in the "Lunch Special."

    Look for "Roast Beef Sand."

    Can you guess what "Sand." is short for?

7. When can you get the "Lunch Special"?

143

Here is a list from a phone book.

TELEPHONES
Buy-a-Phone Co. 281 Park Ave 810-0245
Day Communications 13 Day Road 142-7800
Highway Phones
  "Buy a phone from us"
    46 Mars Hwy 207-3010
    838 Mars Hwy 416-6440
Phone City Inc.
  "The largest phone store in North Town"
    782 Ridge Rd 400-2753

TV SALES
Art's' TV Heaven 280 Mars Hwy 207-7679
Picture Town 246 Park Ave 810-4921
TV City
  "We buy used TV's"
    29 Day Rd 142-4680

1.   Are there any headings in this list?

     How can you tell?

2.   In what kind of order are the names listed?

3.   Look for "Day Communications" in the list.

     What does this store sell?

     How can you tell?

4.   Look for "Picture Town" in the list.

     What does this store sell?

     How can you tell?

5.   You want to sell your TV.

     Look at the list.

     Is there a store that will buy your TV?

6.   Why do you think there are two phone numbers under
       "Highway Phones"?

Here is a list.

TOP TEN SONGS

This Week	SONG/Artist	Last Week
1	GET THE BEAT / The Bugs	3
2	DON'T GO HOME / Al White	2
3	TELL ME NOW / Sue Turner	4
4	YOU'VE GOT STYLE / The Top Dogs	1
5	CAN YOU FIND THE TIME? / A.J. Bacon	6
6	LOOK OUT / The Jane Jones Group	5
7	THE CHICKEN SONG / The Bob Burger Band	7
8	YOU DON'T UNDERSTAND / Ida North	10
9	THE LAST LUNCH / The Five Men	9
10	I CAN'T GET AWAY / P.J. Downs	8

1. What are the things in this list?

   How can you tell?

2. What do the headings at the top of the list tell you?

3. In what order are the names listed?

4. What do the numbers at the right mean?

APPENDIX: Unit Outlines and Word Lists

This book is a guide to reading. To be most effective, the material presented in this book should be supplemented by material that a student may encounter in everyday life. The student should take the points raised in this book and see how they apply in the real world. In this way, the strategies and skills that are pointed out in this book will not be learned in a vacuum.

On the following pages, you will find a rough outline for each unit in this book (with the exception of the review units). The outlines contain the following information:

- general objective of the unit
- a list of new words used in the unit
- the total number of different words used in the unit
- suggested preview activities
- suggested post-unit activities

You can use this information any way you choose. You can use it to supplement an existing lesson plan, or you can use it as an outline for a lesson plan. You may want to revise or recast the suggested activities to fit the special interests or needs of students. The most important thing to do is to place the material in this book within the context of the student's experiences and expectations. Get the student to relate the things in this book to what he may see in the course of a day. Have the student apply the strategies and skills to things that he wants to read. A student will come to understand more about reading by looking at things that interest him rather than by practicing skills and strategies only within the context of a single book.

A NOTE ABOUT THE WORD LISTS

New words that are introduced in a unit appear in the word list for that unit. There are only two kinds of words that are not listed in the word lists: proper names and difficult words that are used only to get the student to use context clues to infer their meaning. Some of the words may appear only once or twice in the book. However, these words contain elements that should be familiar to the student (such as <u>listen</u> on page 48). Nouns and verbs that have their plurals or singulars formed by adding <u>s</u> are listed only once.

147

UNIT 1   (pages 1–5)

Objective: The student looks at pictures and symbols on signs and analyzes them for meaning.

Number of different words used in unit: 46

WORD LIST

a	has	on	their
about	have	out	them
another	here	own	these
are	how	picture(s)	think
at	in	place	this
blanks	is	putting	trying
but	it	road	use
can	list	sign(s)	what
do	looking	some	words
does	mean(s)	tell(s)	you
don't	most	the	your
fill	not		

Preview activities: Talk about signs. Where does one find them? Do all signs have words on them? Ask students to think of some signs that have no words on them. You may want to bring up such things as traffic lights, arrows, and familiar company logos. If it's possible, bring in some newspaper or magazine clippings of wordless symbols or logos.

Post-unit activities: Ask students to find examples of symbol signs or logos. Have the students discuss what the signs mean and how they can tell what they mean.

UNIT 2   (pages 6–13)

Objective: The student looks at words on signs and sees that words can repeat the meaning of a picture or symbol or can add information to the meaning of the picture or symbol.

Number of different words used in unit: 65

Number of new words used in unit: 23

WORD LIST

and	name	same	they
fish	next	sell(s)	thing
for	no	sometimes	turn
if	one	store	where
many	print	store's	yes
mile	right	telephone	

Preview activities: You may want to lead into this lesson by going back to the "no smoking" symbol on page 2. Discuss the idea that words are often used to repeat the message ("NO SMOKING") of this symbol. Sometimes words are used to add to the message (such as "NO SMOKING ON THIS BUS").

Post-unit activities: Discuss the idea that a symbol or picture can't always tell you everything you need to know. Use an arrow as an example. The arrow points in a direction. But can you always figure out what the arrow is for without having something else (such as words) to explain it?

UNIT 3   (pages 14–23)

Objective: The student looks at how pictures, shapes, and physical placement can help to unlock the meanings of unfamiliar words on signs. The student uses these context clues to interpret signs.

Number of different words used in unit: 64

Number of new words used in unit: 17

WORD LIST

all	good	other	stop
clue(s)	know	please	there
danger	may	shape	way
flowers	of	sign's	window
give(s)			

Preview activities: Focus on some familiar signs, such as "stop" signs or store logos. Ask the students if they have ever "read" a familiar sign without actually reading the word. (Example: You drive down the road and see in the distance a red sign that has eight sides and white letters on it. Do you know what the sign says without reading the word?)

Post-unit activities: Continue to discuss such clues as the color, shape, or physical placement of a sign. You may want to pose the following questions:
- If you see a sign above a store front, what is the sign probably telling you?
- Are there any other signs that you can "read" just by looking at the color or shape?

UNIT 5   (pages 27–32)

Objective: The student looks at similarities between signs and simple ads. The student begins to apply the skills used in analyzing signs for meaning to simple ads.

Number of different words used in unit: 68

Number of new words used in unit: 18

WORD LIST

ad(s)	free	sale	to
be	get	say	used
belts	like	show	who
buy	safely	something	why
find	safety		

Preview activities: Ask students to think about and discuss advertisements. Where do ads appear (TV and radio, newspapers, fliers, etc.)? Why are ads used (to sell things, to announce things, as a public service, etc.)?

Post-unit activities: Ask students to think about pictures in ads. How can pictures help to make the meaning of an ad clear? (You may want to refer students back to the "Zippy" ad on page 27. In this ad, only the picture gives the clue that "Zippy" is a dog food.)

UNIT 6   (pages 33–40)

Objective: The student looks at how context (a picture or other words) can be used to determine the meaning of an unfamiliar word and then uses the context clues to determine the meaning of ads; the student also looks at how context can change the meaning of a word.

Number of different words used in unit: 71

Number of new words used in unit: 14

WORD LIST

an	from	now	soda
bugs	great	or	taste(s)
coffee	kill	soap	we
cup	makes		

Preview activities: Discuss some common brand names of products. Ask students how they know what the product is (shape or size of container, past experience with the product, etc.). Can the name of the product have another meaning if it were used in a different way?

Post-unit activities: Ask students to look for and bring in some picture ads. Have them discuss why the pictures are used and how the pictures make the ideas in the ads clearer.

UNIT 7 (pages 41-48)

Objective: The student looks at how to use words, pictures, and other context clues to find the main point of an ad and then applies the clues to find the main point.

Number of different words used in unit: 76

Number of new words used in unit: 21

WORD LIST

add	driving	main	smoke
ad's	each	point	then
answer(s)	important	questions	three
drink	life	radio	TV
drinking	listen	reason	up
drive			

Preview activities: Ask students to interpret the meaning of the words "main point" or "main idea." How does a person look for the main point of something? Why is the main point important?

Post-unit activities: Ask students to watch a TV show. Ask them to think about the main point of the show as they watch it. Then have them talk about the show. How did they figure out the main point? What kinds of clues led them to the main point?

UNIT 9 (pages 52-59)

Objective: The student looks at why lists are used, how they are used, and how information can be organized in a list.

Number of different words used in unit: 110

Number of new words used in unit: 32

WORD LIST

arrow(s)	go	milk	street
burger	group	north	third
butter	hats	our	ties
come	heaven	save	town(s)
easier	highway	shoes	understand
east	let	socks	us
easy	listed	south	want
eggs	men's	straight	world

Preview activities: Point out an example of a sign or an ad that contains a list. Ask students to think about why the list is used. Does the list make it easier to find something? (To reinforce the idea that lists can make something easier to read, you may want to put your example list into a prose style. Then ask students which is easier to read and understand. See page 53 for a model for this activity.)

Post-unit activities: Ask students to think of other kinds of road signs that contain lists (such as mileage signs or certain kinds of "no parking" signs). How is the list in the sign organized? Does the list make the sign easier to read? You may want to construct an example of such a sign and ask students questions about it. (Example: Draw a "no parking" sign that contains a list of days and times during which parking is not permitted. (See page 139 for a model.) Then ask such questions as: "It is Friday. The time is 10:30 AM. Can you park by this sign?")

UNIT 10   (pages 60–68)

Objective: The student looks at how context clues (such as a heading or physical placement) can be used to determine the main point of a list and then applies the clues to find the main point of lists.

Number of different words used in unit: 101

Number of new words used in unit: 18

WORD LIST

cake	heading	races	sugar
can't	hold	salt	that
day	mall	shop	today
flour	movies	songs	top
food(s)	need		

Preview activities: Review the points covered in Unit 7 (finding the main point of an ad). You may want to refer the students back to the ads on pages 55 and 57 and ask them to use the clues to find the main point of each list.

Post-unit activities: Have a student find or make up a list. Ask the other students to figure out the main point of the list. You may also want to present students with a list that does not have a clear main point. Ask them to figure out how the main point could be made clearer (i.e., add a title, add a picture, etc.).

UNIT 11   (pages 69–78)

Objective: The student looks at how the organization of a list can be used to find specific details in the list and then applies the knowledge of organization to find specific details in lists.

WORD LIST

above	grade	news	rates
baseball	guys	number(s)	read
cab	home	order	start
channel(s)	killer	part(s)	talk
comedy	large	PM	time
company	lowest	price(s)	together
dozen	much	put	under
drama	music	quart	with

Preview activities: Bring in a list of TV shows from a local newspaper and show it to the students. Ask them if they have used such a list. Why might they use the list? How would they use it? What do the numbers in the list mean? You may want to preview such specialized vocabulary as comedy, drama, and talk show. These words are not crucial to the students' understanding of the unit, but they do appear in the unit. You may also want to check to make sure that each student understands the time designation "PM."

Post-unit activities: Ask students to look for and bring in lists that appear in newspapers. Discuss the lists with the students. What is the main point of each list? What kind of information is in each list? How would you use the list to find something?

UNIT 13   (pages 83–93)

Objective: In the context of reading a menu, the student looks at how to use classification headings to find specific details. The student also looks at how to use context clues to unlock the meaning of an unfamiliar heading or an unfamiliar word in a list.

Number of different words used in unit: 157

Number of new words used in unit: 57

WORD LIST

also	diner	it's	sandwich
any	duck	kind(s)	sausage
bacon	example	long	served
beef	flounder	lunch	short
beefsteak	French	made	side
below	fried	menu	soup
cheese	fries	must	special
cheeseburger(s)	guess	open	stands
cheesecake	ham	pea	steak

chef's	hamburger	pick	style
chicken	hours	pie	turkey
could	house	plain	two
cream	ice	roast	when
cupcake	idea(s)	salad	would
dessert			

<u>Preview activities</u>: Ask students if they are familiar with menus. What is a menu? Where would you find one? What kind of information is on a menu? (Note: There are two reasons for the relatively high number of new words in this unit. Most of the new words are words that often appear on menus. Also, several of the new words are compound words. You may want to preview the specialized vocabulary that appears on menus before you begin the unit. The exercise on page 93 involves compound words.)

<u>Post-unit activities</u>: Ask students to look for and bring in price lists that have headings in them. Have the students discuss these kinds of lists. Why are the headings used? Do they help to unlock the meanings of unfamiliar words? Do they help to locate specific details?

UNIT 14   (pages 94–105)

<u>Objective</u>: The student looks at how simple tables are organized; the student uses this knowledge of organization to find both the main point and specific details in simple tables.

<u>Number of different words used in unit</u>: 106

<u>Number of new words used in unit</u>: 39

WORD LIST

asks	fat	more	ride
away	finding	non-diet	second
beat	fruit	non-fat	serving
beer	grams	nonfood	size
black	hard	nonstop	skim
bus	help	ounces	TV's
calories	inch	page	until
color	last	protein	what's
diet	line	punch	white
down	looked		
eat			

<u>Preview activities</u>: Ask students if they can remember coming across a list that had a lot of numbers in it. Clip a simple table from a newspaper or magazine and present it as an example. Ask the students if they can think of reasons for the numbers' being put into columns. (Note: This unit contains some nutrition tables. Specialized vocabulary used in the tables includes diet, non-diet, calories, protein, fat, ounces, grams, and serving. You may want to preview the specialized vocabulary before beginning the unit.)

Post-unit activities: Ask students to find and bring in tables from newspapers or magazines. Have the students look at some of the tables and discuss them. You may want to suggest parts of a newspaper in which tables usually appear (i.e., the sports section, the weather report, etc.).

UNIT 15   (pages 106–113)

Objective: The student looks at what timetables are and how they are organized; the student uses this knowledge of organization to find specific details in the timetable.

Number of different words used in unit: 129

Number of new words used in unit: 25

WORD LIST

across	Co. (Company)	No. (Number)	should
after	goes	noon	St. (Street)
AM	happen	oak	supposed
Ave. (Avenue)	here's	park	timetable
avenue	Hwy. (Highway)	Rd. (Road)	train
before	leaves	reading	whole
closest			

Preview activities: Bring in a simple timetable and discuss it with the students. Ask them to analyze how the timetable is set up. What do the headings tell you? What do the times tell you? (Note: The student begins to deal directly with abbreviations in this unit. You may want to discuss what abbreviations are and how they are used before you begin the unit.)

Post-unit activities: Have students look for tables that are similar to the timetable used in this unit. (A mileage chart from a road map is one such table.) Discuss the organization of the tables, and ask some questions that require students to find specific details in the tables.

UNIT 17   (pages 121–129)

Objective: The student looks at how items in a list may be organized; particular stress is placed on alphabetical order as a way to organize items.

Number of different words in unit: 149

Number of new words used in unit: 16

WORD LIST

added	as	juice	meaningful
almost	between	least	only

alphabet	cost(s)	letter(s)	questionable
alphabetical	four	meaning	understandable

Preview activities: Discuss alphabetical order. What does "alphabetical order" mean? When is it used? Give examples of lists that are put in alphabetical order (i.e., the telephone book, a dictionary, etc.). (Note: Make sure that students know the sequence of the alphabet before beginning the unit.)

Post-unit activities: Refer the students back to some of the lists they've already used. Have them identify the method of organization in the list (if there is any). (Example: Have them look at the timetable on page 106. How are the headings organized? How are the times organized?)

UNIT 18   (pages 130–137)

Objective: The student looks at how to scan an alphabetized list for a specific detail; the student applies this scanning technique to find specific details in a phone book listing.

Number of different words used in unit: 145

Number of new words in unit: 32

WORD LIST

bake	department	listing(s)	records
book	dept. (department)	live	recreation
Ch. (Channel)	fire	new	services
chief	floor	newspaper	social
city	hall	office(s)	suppose
civil	health	pg. (page)	traffic
court	hrs. (hours)	phone	U.S.
deeds	largest	police	using

Preview activities: Bring in a local phone book or a clipping from a phone book. Show it to the students and discuss it. What information is put into a phone listing? Is the information put in any kind of order? How are the names listed? You may also want to discuss the use of guide words to find the page on which a word or name may be listed. (Note: Having students make up an alphabetical order list has been purposefully avoided in this unit. Such an activity would require students to use skills not covered in this book.)

Post-unit activities: Have students look for and bring in the classified ad section of a newspaper. Have them look at the organization of this section. Point out the different ways in which the section is organized (by topic and in alphabetical order). Draw the students' attention to some of the more common abbreviations that appear in the ads. What do the abbreviations stand for? Have them look at the context of the ad for clues that will help them determine the meaning of the abbreviation.